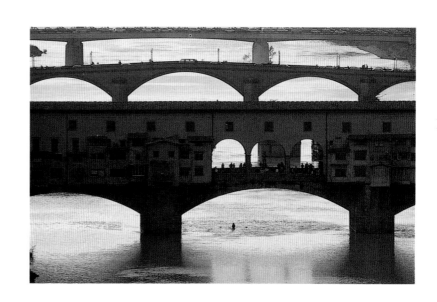

All the photographs in this book were taken by
Giulio Veggi with the exception of the following:

**Franco Nucci:**
pages 88, 89, 90-91.

Printed and bound in Singapore.

First published in English in 1991 by
Tiger Books International PLC, London.
ISBN 1-85501-172-7

Translated by
Patricia Borlenghi

Edited by
Heather Thomas

# INSIDE
# FLORENCE

TEXT
LUISA TSCHABUSHNIG

DESIGN
PATRIZIA BALOCCO

**TIGER BOOKS INTERNATIONAL**

S ome cities arouse excitement and a passionate response in their visitors but Florence evokes composure and dignity. Its magnificent treasures and architectural purity, its countless churches, museums and galleries can be overwhelming at first, and many people find it difficult to take and absorb this visual bombardment from the past.

The Piazza della Signoria, Ponte Vecchio and the cathedral (Duomo) are famous all over the world, and are easily recognisable by any tourist, but you have to look further than the most obvious symbols of the city to discover its true character and essence. Palaces, cathedrals, churches and houses, they all harmonize with each other and integrate within the city, not as isolated monuments of the past but as living entities of the present. Even Dante, in the thirteenth century, pointed out that there was no place in the world as lovely as Florence.

Florence, or *Florentia* as it was called by the Romans, was founded in 59 BC by Julius Caesar as a colony for Roman army veterans, and its original street plan can still be seen in the grid system of blocks that criss-cross each other in the centre of the city. From AD 570 Florence was ruled by the Lombards until it came under Carolingian rule in the ninth century. Florence continued to flourish as the foremost city in Tuscany, particularly under its enlightened eleventh-century ruler Countess Matilda, who encouraged the development of the great medieval guilds and the prosperous textile industry. The city itself prospered and became an important centre for banking and finance, and in 1138 it was proclaimed a self-governing city republic. But despite its new-found wealth there were recurring feuds and conflicts between the merchants, the

guilds and the old nobility, and this grew into the celebrated feuding between the Guelph and Ghibelline parties. At the end of the thirteenth century, under a new governing body of merchants, bankers and guilds, the city embarked on an ambitious building programme that was to change the face of Florence and create the most beautiful city in Tuscany, if not the whole of Italy. It was during this period that work on the Duomo, the Piazza della Signoria and many famous Florentine churches was started.

This heralded a new golden age in Florence's history. Dante Alighieri wrote his immortal masterpiece, *The Divine Comedy*, and Boccaccio composed *The Decameron*. The way lay open for the rise of the Medici family and an artistic revival under the direction of such masters as Giotto, which led to the most momentous and creative period in European history – the Renaissance – in which Florence played a leading role. Under Lorenzo the Magnificent (1449-1492), the most famous of all the Florentine princes, the city's economy and the arts flourished. A true Renaissance man – skilful politician and diplomat, patron of the arts and the model for Machiavelli's *Prince* – Lorenzo presided over a unique period in European culture. During the fifteenth and sixteenth centuries, Florence underwent a physical renaissance under the genius of Brunelleschi, Ghiberti, Donatello and Cellini, while Botticelli, Uccello and, later, Leonardo and Michelangelo contributed some of the world's greatest works of art.

This was an incomparable period in Florence's history. Many old and unfinished buildings were decorated and embellished in the new styles. Brunelleschi crowned the cathedral with its revolutionary dome; Alberti finished its Gothic marble facade in

*8 The Gothic Campanile beside the Cathedral was designed by Giotto and work started on it in 1334. Andrea Pisano continued his work, and it was later completed by Francesco Talenti who decorated it with sculptural reliefs symbolizing the beliefs and philosophies of the medieval world. If you have the stamina, you can climb the 414 stairs to the top for a spectacular view of the city.*

true Renaissance style; Ghiberti embellished the doors of the Romanesque Baptistery; while Ammannati and Donatello supplied an abundance of magnificent sculptures and fountains. Florence was transformed into one of the world's most truly beautiful cities. However, by the end of the sixteenth century, the Medicis' power was in decline, and the Grand Dukes of Tuscany took over their mantle. With the recurring plagues, the collapse of the wool trade, and the stagnation in Florentine banking and finance, the city's golden age came to an end. In 1737 it fell under the domination of the Austrian Hapsburgs and the Lorraine dynasty, and during the nineteenth century it became a prescribed stop for the sons of the British nobility embarking on the Grand Tour of classical and renaissance European art and architecture. Under the Risorgimento, once again Florence regained its prominent status, albeit briefly, when in 1865 it became the capital of the new united Italian kingdom. King Victor Emmanuel moved into the Pitti Palace, while the first Italian parliament met in the Palazzo Vecchio. However, in 1870 Rome was captured by the Italians and Florence's brief flash of glory was over.

In World War II, all the original bridges except the Ponte Vecchio were destroyed on Hitler's orders, but miraculously most of the city's great and artistic treasures survived. The worst damage was done in 1966 when the River Arno burst its banks and it took a sustained international effort and the world's best art experts to restore the city and its treasures, many of which were submerged under flood waters. However, Florence proved once again its natural instinct for survival against the odds, and today it is the best preserved example of the Italian Renaissance.

9 The daring dome of Brunelleschi is a testament to his engineering skills. Its 138-foot diameter and great height made the normal building methods of the time with wooden scaffolding impossible, so Brunelleschi conceived a brilliant double-walled system whereby supporting bricks were laid in a self-supporting spiral which had no need of buttresses or scaffolding.

10-11 This classic view of Florence from the Piazzalè Michelangelo shows the many bridges that cross the Arno which flows right through the heart of the city. The Ponto Vecchio is the sole remaining bridge from medieval times. All the other bridges were destroyed in World War II by the retreating German army and have since been replaced by new ones.

12-13 The Ponte Vecchio is probably the best known of all the sights of Florence. It has been lined with goldsmiths' and jewellers' shops since 1593 when the Medici Grand Duke Ferdinando I evicted the butchers and blacksmiths and decreed that henceforth only more upmarket jewellers would be permitted to trade there. The present bridge with its three stone arches was erected in 1345 to replace an earlier wooden construction which was swept away in a flood.

*14 The river banks were once lined with grim walls and defensive towers, but from the fifteenth century onwards, they were replaced with patrician palaces with splendid decorated facades. These golden palaces, often adorned with romantic statuary, are inherently beautiful and help perpetuate the architectural styles of the past.*

*15 Brunelleschi's dome was admired greatly by Leon Battista Alberti who described it as a 'great structure ascending up to the sky and large enough to enclose the entire population of Tuscany in its shadow'. It is still one of the most wonderful achievements of the Florentine Renaissance and dominates the city.*

16 From the top of Giotto's campanile, you are treated to an incomparable view of the historic city centre. There are three tiers of windows in the bell-tower, and the facade is decorated elaborately with niches lined with pink marble.

*17 Alberti's beautiful facade of the Dominican church of Santa Maria Novella is seen here from behind one of the two obelisks set on turtles around which carriages once raced each other in the Piazza Santa Maria in the 1700s. The bell-tower, built in the 1330s, was once used as a watch tower for locating city fires.*

17

18 Leon Battista Alberti's marble decoration of the upper floor of the church of Santa Maria Novella displayed true architecutural invention and became the model for many Italian Renaissance churches. The triangular pediment and inscribed frieze gave birth to a new era in Renaissance architecture but, in fact, reflected the classical styles of antiquity.

19 The beautiful domes of the Duomo and the church of San Lorenzo are distinguished by their red brickwork and white marble, and are the key elements in the Florentine panorama.

*I*n the heart of the old city, rising up from the Piazza del Duomo, is the Cathedral of Santa Maria del Fiore, known to the locals as the Duomo. It is not only the fourth largest church in the world but also one of the most beautiful. Beneath Brunelleschi's glorious dome, which heralded a new age of Renaissance architecture, and Giotto's soaring Gothic campanile, is a fine Italian Gothic interior – serene yet austere – where Savonarola preached and railed against the vanities of his time. However, it is the dome that is the Cathedral's greatest achievement. This amazing example of engineering brilliance was started in 1420 and has become the most easily recognisable symbol of Florence. It consists not just of one dome but of two – an interior dome within an exterior dome linked by ribbing and interlocking courses of bricks. This was to become the model for the gigantic cupola of St Peter's in Rome. Graceful, sublime and dignified, the dome soars above the Cathedral and the city, and can be seen for miles around. It is one of the great triumphs of renaissance architecture, and you can climb to the top of its lantern and experience a wonderful panoramic view of the city and the Tuscan hills. The facade of the Duomo is inlaid with distinctive green, white and black marble in geometric patterns, which became the model for hundreds of other churches all over Italy.

A short distance away from the Duomo is the twelfth-century octagonal Baptistery, one of the oldest buildings in Florence and affectionately referred to by Dante as 'bel San Giovanni'. The austere Romanesque church has three bronze doors, two of which were designed and made by Ghiberti and were called the 'Gates of Paradise' by none other than the great Michelangelo himself. The interior of the cupola is decorated with glittering thirteenth-century mosaic tiles but it is the doors that are the Baptistery's most memorable and beautiful feature. Depicting scenes from the Old Testament and the life of Christ, they took Ghiberti forty-nine years to finish. While you are in the piazza, visit the Cathedral Museum at its east end with Donatello's statue of Mary Magdalen and Michelangelo's *Pieta* (not the famous sculpture in Rome). Then leave the sacred monuments and churches for the bustling streets outside and head towards the Piazza San Lorenzo and its magnificent church, the interior of which was designed by the great Brunelleschi as a result of a commission by the Medici in 1420. From outside, the church looks very rough and unprepossessing but inside it is a triumph of Renaissance design. The classical purity of the naves with their elegant stone columns and the harmony of its proportions are unparalleled. It is almost as though the whole interior has been sculpted out of stone. Here you will find the tombs of the Medici – Cosimo, Piero and Giovanni – as well as Donatello himself. The pulpits, cast in bronze, were designed and sculpted by Donatello but were raised onto columns making it difficult to appreciate their detailed workmanship. Through the left transept you pass into Brunelleschi's Old Sacristy, regarded by many art historians as one of the finest examples of early Renaissance architecture. However, from the rear of the church you can proceed to the New Sacristy, designed by Michelangelo as another Medici burial chamber – for Lorenzo the Magnificent and Giuliano. Michelangelo also designed the Laurentian Library which can be reached via the cloisters through an ante-room, which has one of the world's most beautiful

*20 The historical centre is the heart of the city, where churches, palaces and statuary are clustered together to create an overall effect of harmonious beauty and perfect symmetry.*

staircases. This sweeping edifice has been compared to a cascade and to the molten lava flowing out of a volcano.

Outside the church, you come back into the twentieth century with a jolt, for in the square outside is a colourful market selling clothes, leathergoods and books. Just down the street is the Mercato Centrale, the city's busy food market selling everything from fresh fruit and vegetables to huge country cheeses and the heads of locally caught wild boar. The market building was designed in 1874 by Mangoni, who was also the architect of the Galleria of Milan. This cast iron and glass building deserves a special visit as it gives you a unique insight into the city and the lives of its people. Under a sixteenth-century loggia is the so-called Porcellino Market which takes its name from the bronze fountain of a wild boar, sculpted by Tacca in 1612. Another little market can be found in the popular area of Santa Croce in Piazza dei Campi, near the beautiful loggia of Vasari. It used to be a fish market but now it's a typical flea market.

Leaving the quarter of San Lorenzo, walk across Via Cavour, with its continuous stream of heavy traffic heading towards the Duomo. This is the daily route of many Florentine students on their way to and from the University. The link between Florence and the cultural and literary world goes back a long way. The cradle of Humanism and the undisputed capital of literature and the arts, Florence is still an important centre of learning and has a powerful intellectual tradition. From the dawn of the *'Dolce Stil Novo'* (sweet new style) as exemplified by Giotto, through the experience of the Renaissance to the nineteenth-century works of Giuseppe Giusti, Florence has continued to exercise its own artistic and intellectual

22 Florence is still a city of crowded, bustling alleyways and tiny streets. The traffic is heavy and the sidewalks narrow, making life tortuous for pedestrians, but most streets and squares are punctuated by beautiful palaces or churches.

23 Piazza della Signoria is dominated by the austere facade of the fortress-like Palazzo Vecchio, now the City Hall, and a living symbol of the city's once glorious past. Arnolfo di Cambio was commissioned in 1299 to design this impressive building.

24-25 The porticoed Piazza della Santissima Annunziata was designed within the strict constraints of Renaissance architectural purity. The simplicity of the white facade is enhanced by the classical stone decoration, creating an unexpected atmosphere of calm and serenity in this noisy, bustling city. The statue of the Grand Duke Ferdinando I was designed by Giambologna.

26-27 By night, the river banks, bridges and the major buildings and monuments are illuminated, especially the Duomo, Giotto's Campanile and the tower of the Palazzo Vecchio.

influence on European culture. Throughout the centuries, many famous cultural institutions have been founded in Florence, including the Accademia della Crusca (literary academy). Now Florentine culture gravitates around the University, the second oldest in Italy, which has several museums and renowned institutions of its own, including such important libraries as the central Biblioteca Nazionale (national Library).

One stop that is essential on every visitor's itinerary is the Piazza della Signoria, a striking square dominated by the Palazzo Vecchio and decorated with some fine examples of Florentine statuary, notably Benvenuto Cellini's bronze *Perseus Holding the Head of the Medusa* which is located in the Loggia. However, the huge Neptune Fountain, designed by Ammannati, is regarded even by the most proud and fiercely patriotic Florentines as an artistic disaster. The Palazzo Vecchio is the most outstanding building in the square – a medieval fortress-like palace with a grim and formidable exterior. Built during the fourteenth century as a meeting-place for the leaders of the guilds, it briefly served as the home of the Italian parliament from 1865 to 1871 and is now the City Hall. Inside the Palazzo, the huge Room of the Five Hundred is decorated with frescos by Vasari and Michelangelo's Victory group of sculptures. Here you will find interiors designed by Vasari, bronzes by Donatello, a fresco by Leonardo and the office of Machiavelli. Outside in the piazza, the fanatical priest Savonarola held the legendary 'bonfire of the vanities' in 1497 when the citizens of Florence were incited to fling their most precious treasures into the flames. Ironically, Savonarola was later burned to death as a heretic on the same spot.

28 The historic centre of the city has changed very little since the sixteenth century when Renaissance Florence was at the peak of its wealth and power.

29 The striking geometric marble patterns decorating the facades of the Baptistery, Duomo and Giotto's Campanile provided a model for other Florentine churches. The green, red and white marble has been arranged in elaborate rectangles and floral decorations making the Duomo resemble 'a cathedral wearing pyjamas' according to one critic!

30-31 *Florence is a mysterious and beautiful city, by day and by night. The Arno is illuminated by the reflections of thousands of lights along its banks, while the Ponte Vecchio is a popular meeting-place in the evenings for the young people of the city.*

*T*he people of Florence are justly proud of their city, its artistic heritage and illustrious past, and seek to safeguard and perpetuate its unique traditions and customs. many of the old festivals, processions and *palios* (free-for-all horse races) have now disappeared into the pages of history, but some traditions still live on in the spirit of the city and keep alive the collective memory that links the present with the glories of the past. Some of the most notable and typically Florentine festivals take place at Easter-time, including the *Scoppio del Carro* (literally translated as the 'explosion of the cart') which starts at noon on Easter Sunday. A mechanical dove, freed from the altar of the Cathedral during mass, starts off a fantastic fireworks display in the piazza outside. The origins of this festival are to be found in the knights returning from the First Crusade. Ascension Day is celebrated in the Cascine Park with the *Festa del Grillo* at which 'singing' crickets are sold imprisoned in tiny cages as good luck charms to be released later. On June 24 is the feast of the patron saint of Florence – San Giovanni. After the usual solemn religious ceremonies, fireworks are traditionally let off in the Piazzale Michelangelo high above the city. On 7 September, the eve of the Feast of the Nativity of the Virgin, the *Festa del Rificolone* is celebrated with a torchlit procession over the Ponte San Niccolo. Also in September is the Bird Fair at the Porta Romana. But perhaps the most famous and certainly the most exciting and colourful of all the uniquely Florentine festivals is the *Calcio*, which is staged over three weekends in June and July for the enjoyment of Florentines and tourists alike. This is an elaborate Renaissance football match played in traditional sixteenth-century costume. The 'kickers' of the four opposing football teams of the oldest districts in the city – San Giovanni, Santa Croce, Santo Spirito and Santa Maria Novella – engage in a series of rough and often violent games which commemorate the battles of medieval Florence. Held in the Boboli Gardens adjacent to the Pitti Palace, the *Calcio* survives from an earlier age and is still supported enthusiastically by the Florentines who identify with and swear allegiance to the four teams. If you are ever in Florence at the time of the *Calcio*, this is a 'must' and not to be missed at any cost.

The Florentine gifts for wit and sarcasm are legendary throughout Italy, and the people have a reputation for being courteous yet proud and enigmatic. Throughout their history, they have somehow always managed to take both sides in any conflict or dispute – and this is a quintessential part of the complex Florentine character even today. Feuding was an intrinsic part of life in medieval and Renaissance Florence, and it continues today in endless disputes over issues such as excessive city traffic, the environment and art restoration. Unlike the popular image of the Italians as a romantic and exuberant Latin people of a passionate temperament, the Florentines are industrious, inventive, sometimes arrogant and always dignified. Many still genuinely believe that they are the élite of Italian cities and society.

The tradition of the Florentine mastery of all arts and crafts runs deep and is etched into the city's history and the people's character. It is not only the home of some of the woirld's greatest ever artists, sculptors, poets and architects, but it is also today a thriving centre for many craftsmen, including jewellers, goldsmiths, embroiderers, bookbinders, ropemakers and

furniture-makers who have their roots in the old artisan traditions of the once powerful medieval guilds. There are many contemporary goldsmiths and jewellers creating exciting new designs of the finest workmanship. There are also leather factories where you can buy a wide range of leathergoods, including handbags, purses, wallets, belts, shoes and clothing. You can also visit the leather school hidden away behind the sacristy of San Croce where apprentices come from all over the world. The traditional Florentine craft of inlaying wood is still practised, and you can buy anything from a picture frame to a table.

Florence plays host to many international exhibitions throughout the year, including craft and fashion shows, and antique, jewellery, fur and knitwear fairs. There is a full calendar of arts and handicrafts events, whichever month of the year it happens to be. The arts are still very much alive and flourishing in the city, and concerts, the ballet, opera, drama and film all play their part on the Florentine cultural scene. In the summer months you can enjoy one of the evening open-air concerts in the Boboli Gardens. The internationally acclaimed concerts of the Maggio Musicale Fiorentina are held in May and June in the Teatro Communale and attract some of the world's greatest musicians and operatic stars. At the same theatre, in the winter months, you can go to the opera and revel in the music of Verdi, Puccini and other celebrated Italian composers. There is also an annual Florence film festival which is held every spring. If you prefer more popular contemporary music, there are several jazz clubs and discothèques, and some excellent piano bars in the best hotels.

*33 In 1400, the holy ceremony made use of a triumphal cart on top of which torches and rockets were lit. This procedure is still followed today and the* Scoppio del Carro *has become one of the great Florentine traditions.*

36-37 The teams are preceded by a splendid procession of flag-wavers, crossbowmen and trumpeters dressed in the colourful, sumptuous costumes of the period. The Calcio has become an exciting spectacle for Florentines and visitors alike.

38-39 The Calcio is a reminder of the feuding factions that opposed each other in medieval Florence, when even Lorenzo de Medici himself was an enthusiastic participant in the sport of 'kicking'.

40-41 The districts of San Giovanni, Santa Croce, Santo Spirito and Santa Maria Novella face each other in a series of eliminating knock-out rounds of frequently violent games of football against the continuous background shouting by each district's supporters.

*T*he Ponte Vecchio, which spans the Arno at its narrowest point, is the oldest bridge in Florence and was once the most important thoroughfare between the two sides of the city built on opposite banks of the river. Built in 1345 to replace the earlier twelfth-century wooden construction which was swept away by flood waters, the Ponte Vecchio is lined with jewellers' shops and is a magnet for visitors to Florence. It was originally the centre for the city's hog butchers after Cosimo de Medici commissioned Vasari to build a covered passageway over the bridge. It became the link between the Palazzo Pitti, where the Medici lived, and the Uffizi, which was their offices. In 1593 Grand Duke Ferdinando I, unable to tolerate the butchers any longer on his daily journey across the bridge, expelled them all and ordered that from henceforth only jewellers and goldsmiths should be permitted to do their business there. And to this day, these are the only trades allowed on the bridge.

The Ponte Vecchio is the only bridge in Florence to survive World War II; the other bridges were destroyed in 1944 by the retreating German armies after the Arno became a defensive line against the advancing Allied armies. Only the Ponte Vecchio was spared by Hitler, but at a cost – the beautiful old houses at either end of the bridge were blown up in order to block the Allied advance with piles of rubble. At sunset, when the Arno flows blood-red and gold under the old stone arches, the Ponte Vecchio looks sublimely beautiful and peaceful.

Sometimes dull and cloudy, at other times blue and clear, the Arno flows serenely through the centre of the city past palaces, churches and elegant villas. The commercial and cultural heart of

Florence sprawls across the right bank, stretching away towards the distant hills of Fiesole. If you cross over the Arno to the left bank, you will enter the district of Oltrarno, which literally means 'beyond the Arno'. Many of the houses here were destroyed during the war but it is now a popular residential district. Only the Pitti Palace remains as a reminder of its former Renaissance glory. Built in 1457 for Luca Pitti, a powerful Florentine banker, the Pitti Palace was acquired by the Medicis in the sixteenth century and later became the official residence of the Grand Dukes of Tuscany. Much later it became the palace of the new kings of Italy, the House of Savoy, after the Risorgimento, but today it is a magnificent complex of museums, which include the Royal Apartments, the Galleria Palatina, the Museo degli Argenti and the Galleria d'Arte Moderna. Most famous of all is the Galleria Palatina with its celebrated collection of sixteenth and seventeenth-century paintings including works by Titian, Rubens, Raphael and Caravaggio. The contemporary Galleria d'Arte Moderna exhibits works by Tuscan painters, Italian Impressionists and Pissarro. Outside and adjacent to the palace are the Boboli Gardens, once the private gardens of the Medici and now a public park. Laid out in formal Italianate style in the sixteenth century, these gardens contain an amphitheatre, and a wealth of statuary, ponds, grottoes and fountains. Ascending from the Pitti palace in a series of tiers is the Medicis' own private amphitheatre. Decorating the gardens are classical Roman statuary together with some Renaissance masterpieces by Giambologna and Tacca. This is a green oasis in the city with magical views of olive trees, Lombardy poplars, vineyards and typically Tuscan villas. Standing here in the peace of

the gardens, surrounded by statues, it feels as though time has stood still and it is easy to visualize those far-off days when Florence was ruled by the Medicis.

Also in the Oltrarno is the Piazza Santo Spirita which has the last church to be designed by Brunelleschi. Completed in 1487 after his death, its interior beauty is well hidden behind an unprepossessing facade. But inside it is a treasure house of paintings and stained glass windows set within a perfectly proportioned building which was designed with mathematical precision. The result is a supremely dignified church of classical colonnades and semicircular chapels all built in Brunelleschi's characteristic pale grey stone – *pietra serena*. To many Renaissance art historians this is perhaps the greatest of all Florence's churches and Brunelleschi's masterpiece.

Nearby in the Brancacci Chapel of Santa Maria del Carmine are some spectacular frescoes by Masolino, Masaccio and Filippino Lippi. They were restored in the 1980s and now you can view them in their true vibrant colours as they were painted. The naturalistic style of *The Expulsion of Adam and Eve* and the feeling for light and perspective in *The Tribute Money* make them a masterpiece of Renaissance painting and set them among the most momentous and greatest frescoes ever painted. You cannot fail but be moved by their great humanity.

*48 The Caffè Gilli is an elegant refuge in the city where you can relax and still enjoy the belle époque atmosphere of the past in modern Florence.*

49 The ceiling of the I Latini restaurant is festooned with cured hams and bunches of garlic. It specializes in traditional Tuscan delicacies which are prepared and served in the time-honored way.

50-51 The streets and the squares of the city centre are crowded with people and traffic all day long, but it is still possible to find green oases of calm where you can relax over a coffee or an aperitivo.

54 The green hills above the city are dotted with sedate villas which are almost completely hidden by trees and surrounded by formal gardens in the classic Italianate style. This graceful villa looks very peaceful but in fact it is only a stone's throw away from the Piazzale Michelangelo.

55 From the dramatic Boboli Gardens which sweep across the hills adjacent to the Pitti Palace, you can get a spectacular view of the city and its most famous churches and palaces.

56 Decorated with distinctive inlaid patterns of green and white marble, the Baptistery is a splendid example of Romanesque architecture and was to influence generations of distinguished architects of the Renaissance, including the great Michelangelo.

*57 The fourteenth-century Romanesque facade of the lower part of the church of Santa Maria Novella is surmounted by a beautiful second floor and pediment designed by Alberti in black and white marble. The 'S' shaped curving scrolls on either side of the upper floor are unprecedented and were copied on churches all over Italy.*

*58 The bronze doors on the north and east sides of the Baptistery are regarded as a masterpiece. They are the work of the renowned Florentine sculptor Lorenzo Ghiberti who spent most of his life creating these 'Gates of Paradise' as they were dubbed by Michelangelo. The south-side doors were designed by Andrea Pisano.*

*T*he spiritual and the worldly sides of life are both to be found in Florence, most notably in the many *palazzi* (palaces) built by ambitious Florentine nobles who wished to ensure their everlasting fame and to establish a new dynasty. The phenomenon of the *palazzo* spread quickly and it soon became a dominant feature of the Renaissance. During this exciting and creative age, when men were involved in a continuous process of discovery, invention and experimentation against the changing face of political and economic fortunes, civil architecture became an enduring theme. The palazzi themselves became a concrete and lasting symbol of the magnificence and wealth of the city's new aristocracy. Thus the unique relationship between the commissioning noble and patron, and the architect was sealed, and the inseparable bond between the Renaissance architect and his noble environment was born.

In 1444, Cosimo de Medici entrusted the works on the Palazzo Medici, the future residence of Lorenzo the Magnificent, to Michelozzo. The magnificence of the project led Luca Pitti, the powerful rival of the Medicis, to commission immediately Brunelleschi to construct an even grander and more monumental palazzo on the slopes of the Boboli hills overlooking the city. The stone used to build the palace was excavated from the very same hill, and you can see the results for yourself today.

Through the efforts of Michelozzo and Brunelleschi, the medieval idea of the 'fortress-house', albeit beautiful and highly decorated, survived. However, the arrival on the Florentine scene of Leon Battista Alberti started a new trend in this upper-class building trade. He introduced a new more classical style which is

59 This detail of the Gothic south door which was completed by Andrea Pisano in 1330 depicts a scene from the life of Saint John the Baptist.

*60 Top:* The most beautiful church on the outskirts of Florence is undoubtedly San Miniato, which was built in 1015. The characteristic green, white and black marble facade was started in 1090 and finished in the twelfth century. The golden eagle of the medieval cloth merchants' guild decorates the roof. It is well worth a visit to admire not only the church but also the view of the panorama of Florence.

*60 Bottom:* The forbidding Bargello was once the residence of the Medici chief of police and later, more infamously, the city prison and torture chamber. Today it is a National Museum and contains a notable collection of sculptures by the great Florentine masters – Michelangelo, Benvenuto Cellini, Giambologna and Donatello.

manifested in the Palazzo Rucellai and the Palazzo Uguccioni in Piazza Signoria. Cosimo I, in his enormous building and renovation programme, favoured the new more self-conscious Mannerist style of Florentine architecture as expressed by Vasari. A typically multi-talented Renaissance genius, Vasari not only designed many buildings of the period but he also was an artist and furniture-maker. A good example of his new multi-faceted approach is to be found in the Palazzo Vecchio where the huge hall, adorned with mythological allegories and historical narratives, celebrates the epic deeds of the house of Medici.

From the most important art gallery in all Italy, the Uffizi Palace, to the smallest of all, Florence's galleries and museums represent a complete manual of art history from classical to modern times and contain a rich cultural heritage. The origins of the Florentine museums' great collections are to be found in the Medici family's magnificent private art collections. Cosimo I undertook the formidable task of gathering together all the family collections and he assigned the works to the Palazzo degli Uffizi, and this work was continued later by Francesco I. The expansion of the gallery and the enrichment of the collections were of common interest to most members of the Medici dynasty. In fact, the Uffizi contains masterpieces from all the periods of Italian painting and also a selection of international art. The richly decorated rooms are embellished with sculpture, statues and classical busts, and Florentine and Flemish tapestries. The outstanding paintings in the collection include such world-famous works as Botticelli's *Primavera* and *Birth of Venus*; Michelangelo's *Holy Family*; Leonardo's *Adoration of the Magi*; Uccello's *Battle of San Romano*;

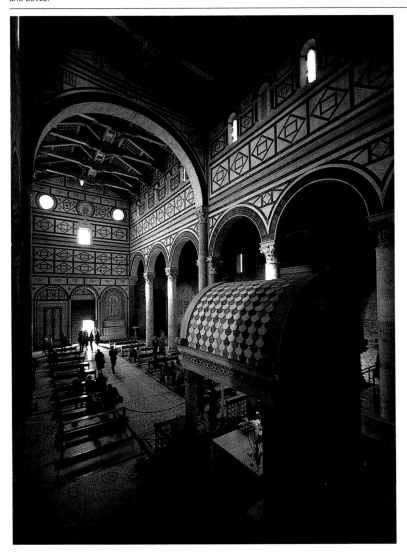

61 The interior of San Miniato is decorated splendidly with inlaid marble. Most notable is the elaborate marble floor created in 1207 and inlaid with the signs of the Zodiac and patterns of lions and doves.

and Caravaggio's *Bacchus*. There are also paintings by Giotto, Martini, Titian, Raphael, Masaccio, Piero della Francesca and by non-Italian painters like Hugo van der Goes and Rembrandt. This is the finest collection of Renaissance art ever assembled and the sheer volume of wonderful paintings that assails the visitor to the Uffizi can be overwhelming even to the most fanatical art-lover. There are guided tours of the Uffizi on offer, or you can just explore it in your own way at your own pace, pausing to admire and enjoy the greatest masterpieces. If you visit the gallery in the summer months, remember that it can get very crowded so it is best to go early in the morning before the crowds descend on it. Afterwards you can relax on the summer terrace of the gallery's bar and rest your aching feet and have a well-earned drink.

At the end of the day after a busy itinerary of galleries, palaces and churches, the city is transformed by the sunset and the palaces and the Arno are bathed in an extraordinary mellow golden light. The cool evenings and the nights have a charm all of their own; the illuminated churches exude a mysterious beauty, and as darkness falls the palazzi and campaniles paint dark shadows on the piazzas. The sidewalk cafés are noisy and crowded in the evenings and muscicians play in the streets and squares. The restaurants and colorful trattoria offer typically Tuscan food and wine with many local delicacies. Robust *antipasto* dishes, pasta in a multitude of sauces, creamy risotto, local game, wild mushrooms and the ubiquitous *bistecca alla fiorentina* can be found on most menus. Accompanied by a glass of the excellent local Chianti, you can treat yourself to some of the best food that Italian cuisine can offer.

62 Brunelleschi's dome and Giotto's campanile complement each other perfectly to create a wonderful example of architectural symmetry.

63 The Cathedral of Santa Maria del Fiore, better known locally as the Duomo, is one of the finest examples of Italian Gothic architecture. Built on the old site of the church of Santa Reparata, the cornerstone was laid in 1294 and the building work was financed by a special property tax. Arnolfo di Cambio was chosen to design the great building but unfortunately he did not live to see the completion of the facade which was finished only in the fourteenth century.

*64-65 The Ponte Vecchio derives some of its charm from the old blocks of houses built on the structure of the bridge itself in variegated shades of cream, ochre and siena which have been kissed by the sun and faded by the centuries.*

66 The marble lantern surmounting the dome of the Cathedral is topped by a bronze globe and golden cross – the fundamental elements of Christian symbolism.

*67 From the Piazzale Michelangelo there is an incomparable view of Florence. In the centre of the square stands a copy of Michelangelo's David. This is a popular tourists' destination, and the square is spoilt somewhat by the proliferation of ice-cream vendors and souvenir shops.*

*68-69 The Florence May Music Festival is one of the oldest and most prestigious musical festivals in Italy, and every year it attracts internationally acclaimed singers, conductors, musicians and soloists.*

*70-71 The Uffizi became part of the public heritage in 1737 when it was donated by Anna Maria Ludovica, the last member of the Medici dynasty. The Botticelli rooms are particularly bewitching, displaying his greatest masterpieces, notably* The Birth of Venus *and* La Primavera, *which was painted in 1478.*

72 The Uffizi is undoubtedly the best gallery in Italy and is renowned throughout the world for its unique collections. It has a magnificent collection of sculptures, particularly classical Greek and Roman marbles.

*73 The gallery's most famous collections are gathered in forty-five rooms on the upper floors. On the ground floor are the remains of the Romanesque church of San Piero Scheraggio with some beautiful frescoes by Andrea del Castagno. Room 18, the octagonal Tribuna, is shown here. Designed by Buontalenti in 1584 to hold the most precious treasures of the Medicis, it has a dome decorated with mother-of-pearl and a pietra dura floor and table.*

74 The Accademia Gallery was founded in 1784 by Grand Duke Pietro Leopoldo to provide examples of art from every period and was enriched greatly in 1873 when many of Michelangelo's works were transferred there.

75 The main attraction of the Galleria dell'Accademia is Michelangelo's gigantic David, sculpted when he was still a young man of twenty-nine, and the largest statue executed since the golden age of Rome. Here also you will find Michelangelo's unfinished Slaves, the Palestine Pieta and Saint Matthew.

76-77 *The courtyard entrance to the Palazzo Vecchio was reconstructed between 1439 and 1454 by Michelozzo and was replastered in 1565 by Vasari for the occasion of Francesco I's marriage. The top floors pay testimony to the splendours of fifteenth-and sixteenth-century Florence and boast a series of rooms with decorated ceilings by the da Maiano brothers which are adorned with sculptures.*

*A*lthough it is surrounded by the Tuscan hills, Florence has comparatively few green parks and open spaces. Apart from the Boboli Gardens, the only other park of note is the Cascine, a long narrow strip of green on the right bank of the Arno. Once it was the dairy farm of the Medici and later it became a hunting park, but it is now a recreation and leisure area with a children's zoo, amusement park, tennis courts, swimming pool, race tracks and even a riding school. Yet it was here that Shelley composed his *Ode to the West Wind*, and his drowned body was subsequently burned on a huge funeral pyre.

To enjoy the best panoramic view of the city you must climb up to Piazzale Michelangelo or the Belvedere Fortress, which was built as a defensive fortification in 1429 to protect Florence against besieging armies. From here, you will experience a fine view of the city, its major buildings, churches, palaces and monuments set against the backdrop of the rolling green Tuscan hills. You will identify easily Brunelleschi's soaring dome of the Cathedral, the Palazzo Vecchio's distinctive tower and the church of Santa Maria Novella. You may also see the largest Franciscan basilica in Italy – the church of Santa Croce. The nineteenth-century Neo-Gothic facade hides an inner Renaissance beauty and some of the finest sculptures and murals in Florence as well as the tombs of some of its most famous sons, including Michelangelo and Machiavelli as well as such famous non-Florentines as Galileo and Rossini. Here also is Donatello's marvellous *Annunciation* in gray *pietra serena,* and his wooden *Crucifix,* a more controversial work which Brunelleschi complained made Christ look like a peasant.

Santa Croce is reputed to have been founded by St Francis

himself, and during repairs of the damage caused by the 1966 flood, the remains of an older thirteenth-century church were discovered on the same site. To the right of the Sanctuary are the Peruzzi and Bardi Chapels decorated with frescoes painted in the 1330s by the legendary Giotto. Restored in 1959, they had been whitewashed over in the eighteenth century, but now their colours and drama have been revealed exposing vividly painted scenes of Saint Francis and Saint John the Baptist. There are also fourteenth-century frescoes by Taddeo Gaddi representing the life of the Virgin Mary. Santa Croce is a veritable treasure trove of sacred and religious art, and although the architecture may appear somewhat austere, its beautiful stained glass windows, statuary, paintings and frescoes make it possibly the most important church in Florence – a sort of Florentine pantheon. When you leave the church, you can cross over the bridge and climb the opposite hill to the Piazzale Michelangelo for the other best views of Florence. But remember as you gaze across this great city of culture and the arts that alongside the most famous sights are hidden a thousand other pockets of rare beauty just waiting to be discovered. Nowhere is the relationship between the sacred and the worldly more eloquently expressed than in Florence's churches and palaces. Florence is unique among the world's great cities: a monument and testament to the new philosophy, the vision and creativity of the Renaissance. It is a phenomenon never again to be repeated, and one that you will never forget.

*80 An elegant marble fountain stands in the centre of the Piazza Santo Spirito. The square is dominated by the sober facade of the church of Santo Spirito which was designed by Brunelleschi.*

*81 The cloisters of San Lorenzo were built in 1457 by Manetti in the style of Brunelleschi and from here you can enter the Biblioteca Laurentiana (the Laurentian Library) which was designed by Michelangelo and founded by Cosimo il Vecchio.*

*82-83 The greenery in the Boboli Gardens, laid out by Tribolo in 1549, is enhanced by the distinctive sculptures and grottoes which are scattered across the terraces, along the avenues and in the ponds.*

*86-87 The Boboli Gardens contain a wealth of statuary, especially fountains. The bronze statue of Neptune, cast by Stoldo Lorenzo in 1568, stands on a rustic rocky island in the centre of the Neptune Pond above the granite basin of the Amphitheatre which came from the Roman baths of Caracalla.*

90-91 The river banks, pictured here under a thick white blanket of snow, look very peaceful framed by the old palazzi against the backdrop of the city skyline.

*92-93 The city is as beautiful by night as it is by day, with the most important buildings and churches illuminated against the dark sky. The Ponte Vecchio is a wonderful elevated pathway which is still busy as it reflects the warm glow of the setting sun and night falls over the city.*

*94-95 The houses and palaces lining the river banks are an inexhaustible source of colours and reflections as the sun sinks behind the Tuscan hills and the Arno becomes a river of graduated pinks and molten gold.*